OPTIONS TRADING CRASH COURSE

HOW TO GET STARTED TRADING OPTIONS ON
INDEX FUNDS (IN A WEEK OR LESS)

John B. Stevenson

Table of Contents

INTRODUCTION 8

CHAPTER 1: WHAT ARE OPTIONS? 10

  ELEMENTS IN OPTIONS TRADES.. 13

    Underlying Asset 13

    Type of Trading Option 14

    Strike Price 14

    Premium Price 15

    Expiration Date 16

    Settlement Option 16

  TYPES OF OPTIONS TRADES... 17

    Calls Options Trading 18

    Puts Options Trading 18

    American Type Options Trading 19

    European Type Options Trading 19

    Market-Traded Options Trading 19

    Over-Counter Options Trading 20

    Employee Shares Options Trading 20

    Settled Cash Options Trading 20

  EXPIRY BASED OPTIONS TRADING TYPES 21

  FUNDAMENTAL SECURITY-BASED OPTIONS TRADING TYPES 22

  EXOTIC TRADING OPTIONS TYPES 23

CHAPTER 2: PROS AND CONS OF OPTIONS 26

  PROS OF TRADING OPTIONS 26

    Potential for Astronomical Profits 27

    Great Risk vs. Reward Consideration 28

    Versatility and Flexibility 28

CONS OF OPTIONS TRADING 29

    Are Options an Easy Task? *30*

CHAPTER 3: UNDERSTAND THE RISKS OF OPTIONS TRADING 34

TIME IS NOT ON YOUR SIDE 35

PRICES CAN MOVE PRETTY FAST 36

NAKED SHORT POSITIONS CAN RESULT IN SUBSTANTIAL LOSSES 37

CHAPTER 4: BINARY OPTIONS 38

THE BENEFITS OF PICKING BINARY OPTIONS 39

HOW TO TRADE BINARY OPTIONS 40

BINARY OPTION TIMEFRAMES 42

    Weekly trading *42*

    Intraday trading *44*

CHAPTER 5: WHEN TO EXIT AN OPTIONS TRADE 46

CHAPTER 6: TECHNICAL ANALYSIS AND ITS BENEFITS 52

    Top-Down Technique *53*

    Bottom-Up Technique *53*

CHARACTERISTICS OF TECHNICAL ANALYSIS 55

THE BENEFITS OF TECHNICAL ANALYSIS IN OPTIONS TRADING 58

    Expert Trend Analysis *58*

    Entry and Exit Points *58*

    Leverage Early Signals *59*

    It Is Quick *59*

    It Gives You a Lot of Information *59*

    You Understand Trends *60*

    History Always Repeats Itself *61*

    Enjoy Proper Timing *62*

    Applicable Over a Wide Time Frame *62*

TECHNICAL ANALYSIS SECRETS TO BECOME THE BEST TRADER 62

    Use More than One Indicator *63*

    Go for Multiple Time Frames *63*

Understand that No Indicator Measures Everything..........................64

Go with the Trend 64

Have the Right Skills 64

Trade with a Purpose...64

Always Opt for High value...65

Be Disciplined...65

Don't Overlook Your Trading Plan 65

Accept Losses..66

Have a Target When You Trade...66

PRICE CHARTS **66**

Line chart...67

Bar chart 67

Candlestick chart 68

Point and figure chart...68

Trend or range 69

CHART PATTERNS TO BE AWARE OF **69**

Flags and Pennants...69

Head Above Shoulders Formation 70

HOW TO APPLY TECHNICAL ANALYSIS **71**

1. Identify a Trend...71

2. Support and Resistance Levels 72

3. Look for Patterns 72

TREND INDICATORS..**72**

Moving Average Crossovers...73

Average Directional Movement- ADX......................................76

Momentum Oscillators..77

Stochastic Oscillator...77

CONCLUSION **82**

OPTIONS TRADING TERMINOLOGY...**84**

Introduction

Options trading is recommended for those who are beginners in investing as well as experts. This book is ideal for beginners as it serves as a crash course/guide about everything you need to know about this subject. It contains vast information and pragmatic examples about options trading and ways to perform it efficiently. Learning about systematically can let you have great amounts of profit. A majority of us still believe that trading refers to exchanging goods and services for money. Mainly, a person buys goods at a lower rate and sells at a higher rate. The same concept extends to options trading, except that it also involves a few more conditions. There are many different conditions to bear in mind, such as the volume of the trades, the finance, the exchange values, etc. We will see all of that in detail.

One significant term associated with options is derivatives. If you have been in the world of stocks for some time, then you will be well aware of this condition and what it brings to the table. At the core of it, derivatives are underlying goods or products that help people earn their incentives. For example, if an apple pie is delicious, then the reason for it will be fresh apples, fresh ingredients, and the chef's skills. Similarly, for a financial instrument to do well, many derivatives should work in its favor and should be obtained at a reasonable price.

This trading depends heavily on the prices of the products or other such conditions. Options trading is nothing but a contract between two or more parties, usually the buyer and the seller.

It is all about providing an option to the buyer that a particular asset can be valuable in the future. The seller of the commodity will get a fee or a small amount of money as a reservation of the option. The seller then guarantees that he will keep the option and sell it in full once the buyer pays the total amount.

CHAPTER 1:

What are Options?

An option is basically an agreement on the underlying shares of stock. It is an agreement to exchange shares at a fixed price over a certain timeframe (they can be bought or sold). The first thing that you should understand about options is the following. Why would someone get involved with the options trading in the first place? Most people come to options trading with the hope of earning profits from trading the options themselves. To truly understand what you are doing, you need to understand why options exist to begin with.

There are probably three main reasons that options on stocks exist. The first reason is that it allows people that have shares of stock to earn money from their investment in the form of regular income. So, it can be an alternative to dividend income or even enhance dividend income. If you own a minimum of 100 shares of some stock, this is a possibility. Then you can sell options against the stock and earn income from that over time intervals lasting from a week to a month, generally speaking.

Obviously, such a move entails some risk, but people will enter positions of that type when the relative risk is low. The second reason that people get involved with options is that they offer insurance against a collapse of the stock. So, once again, an option involves being able to trade shares of the stock at a fixed price that is set at the time the contract is originated. One type of contract allows the buyer to purchase shares, the other allows the buyer to sell shares. This allows people who own large numbers of shares to purchase something that provides protection of their investment that would allow them to sell the shares at a fixed price if their stock was declining by huge amounts on the market. So, the concept is exactly like paying insurance premiums. It is unclear how many people actually use this in practice, but this is one of the reasons that options exist.

The way this would work would be that you pay someone a premium to secure the right to sell them your stock at a fixed price over some time frame. Then if the share price drops well below that degree to price, you would still be able to sell your shares and avoid huge losses that were occurring on the market.

The third reason that I would give for the existence of options is that it provides a way for people to decide to purchase shares of stock at the prices that they find attractive, which are not necessarily available on the market. So, there is a degree of speculation here. But let us just say that a particular stock you are interested in is trading at $100 a share. Furthermore, let us assume that people are extremely bullish on the stock, and they are expecting it to rise by a great deal in the coming weeks. Maybe, it is the earnings season.

During earnings season, stock can move by huge amounts. But before the earnings call, nobody knows whether the stock is going to go up or down or by how much it is going to move. An options contract could allow someone to speculate and set up a situation where they could profit from a huge move upward without having to actually invest in the stock. So in that situation, if the stock declined instead, they would not be out of much money.

Just for an example, let us say they buy an options contract that allows them to purchase the shares (of the stock currently at $100) for $102, and the option costs two dollars per share. So, the stock would have to go to $104 or higher to make it worth it.

Typically, options contracts involve 100 shares. So, if the speculator bets wrong, the most they would be out would be $200.

Let us just say, after the earnings call, the share price jumps to $120. The speculator can exercise the option, which means they buy the shares at $102 per share. Then they can sell the stock on the market at the price of $120 per share. Considering the investment to buy the options contract, that basically leaves them with the sixteen $16 per-share profit. Now, you might say well why didn't they just buy the shares that $100 a share?

The reason is if they did that, they would actually be exposed to the stock to the fullest extent possible. Like we said, earnings calls can go both ways. Just recently, Netflix announced that it lost subscribers. In after-hours trading alone, the stock lost $43 per share. So, in our little example, we could say that the stock dropped instead of gaining, let us say to $80 per share. In that case, our speculator would have been in a major point of pain had they actually purchase the shares ahead of time. By doing the option instead, they set themselves up for profit while only risking a $200 loss. And it turns out that there are strategies you can use with options to profit no matter which way the stock moves. So, I did not want to get too far ahead of we, but an experienced options trader would have set up a trade designed to earn profits either way.

Elements in Options Trades

Underlying Asset

An underlying asset can be described as the financial assets in which prices of a derivative are based upon. In this case, the derivative will be options. It is a financial instrument that can price a specific asset. Good elucidation can be depicted by an option on a certain stock, say XYZ. An options trader has the right to either sell or buy the option at an agreed strike option price, which has a limited time. An underlying asset can spot the item being the aim of the contract. This helps an individual to be able to value the contract he or she is signing up for. The underlying asset tends to give participants of the security that is needed by both parties.

The price of the contract an individual is participating in is often determined by the type of asset being traded. The contract of an options trade is supposed to have two parties who are either buying or selling the underlying assets. Let's expound on the stock options as the underlying asset. If an individual has the potential of purchasing one hundred shares of a certain company for one hundred American dollars, this will be the determinant of the value possessed by the option contract. An underlying asset can be a market index.

Type of Trading Option

The current financial market has seen numerous types of options being traded. The contract agreed by option trading parties is supposed to have a clear indication of which type of option is being traded. The types of options that are known in the current world tend to categorize and named depending on the varied features they pose. People across the globe are familiar with two types of options. Calls and puts options are popular in the financial markets.

Puts option gives a trader the ability to sell underlying assets. On the other hand, call options give an individual trading option the right to purchase an underlying asset. There are two common types of options that have been featured in the options contracts are known as the American and European options.

Entering into a contract of American options allows a financial trader to be able to trade his or her underlying assets between the date e or she had purchased them to the date they are bound to be invalid. On the other hand, trade options contracts that contain European options bound an individual to perform his or her trades on the edge of the expiry time.

Strike Price

The presence of a strike price is a common phenomenon in the trade of options. It can be described as a major component when it narrows down to penning down of an option contract. Options such as calls and puts are heavily dependent on this factor. Its critical nature can be shown by an option trader who needs the call options. It is important because it determines the value possessed by the option. Several people have familiarized strike prices with a different name, which is known as the exercise price.

The criticality of this component of the contract makes it one of the components that are talked about earlier between the contractual parties before them entering an agreement or contract. It can inform an investor or trader what the trader what in-the-value money is supposed to be achieved. The underlying price value of the traded assets is supposed to be lower than the strike price. In many cases, the strike price is always affected by the time frame of the contracts. One is supposed to remember that strike price operates on fixed amounts that can be converted to dollars. However, they vary depending on the contract and individual has.

Premium Price

The premium can be described as the price an option buyer in a contract pays the seller of the option. Terms of an option contract state that the amount is always paid upfront. It is always important for a trader to always remember that this component of a contract is not refundable. The rule extends itself to the side that one cannot be refunded his or her money even if the contract has been exercised. The premium quotation in a contract is always done in a certain way for efficiency. The most common way across the globe entails the quotation of option in the foundation of shares, which is termed per share basis. The amount of premium is always affected by several variables before it is agreed on. The common determinants of premium prices are swayed by three major factors that are the volatility value of the option price. It is timing and intrinsic value.

Expiration Date

One can easily understand the term expiration date of a contract as the last day, he or she has the right to exercise either buying or selling the underlying financial instruments. A contract is termed worthless in moments the expiration date has passed. The expiration date tends to differ depending on the type of contract an individual has entered this despite the general principle of the contract being worthless after the last days. A contract using the American style of option trading gives an options trader the right to be able to trade his or her options from the date he or she purchased them to the day they expire. However, European sty trading fixes an individual to only performing his or her trades on the last days of contract expiration.

Settlement Option

The settlement of options can be described as the process by which the holder and writer of an options contract resolve and exercise the terms stated. The process entails the participation of two parties in the trade of options, and it differs depending on the options one has decided to trade. It can be illustrated with both the calls and puts options. In call options, it involves a holder paying the writer of the option. This is the reverse in the puts options since the holder of the options is the one selling them.

Types of Options Trades

Several forms of options are widely exchanged. These alternatives may be divided into various categories about the features they contain. There are two main types of options to the brad sense. The two options are recognized as options for calls and puts. A call option does have the ability to entitle a buyer to buy a financial asset. But on the other side, options confer the ability to sell an asset on an individual. There's a clear distinction used to categorize the option, which is either they 're either European or American style.

The notion that you may end up with is that the categorization is based on geographic location, which isn't really the case. The real reality is that regardless of where the agreement can be performed, registration is achieved. The option classification process goes a little further to utilizing the method used to classify them in trading.

Other techniques used to differentiate the current types of options provide the insurance policy to which they relate and the cycle of expiration they contain. This expands personal observations around the globe to many forms of choices. To grasp the idea of trading options, these sorts of options may be well explained to an individual.

Calls Options Trading

These forms of options are defined by granting the opportunity to purchase the negotiated commodity at a future date to a person. The properties that are acquired appear to have a premium previously settled upon.

There are some instances when a person will make a decision on a property. The most popular scenario is where one theorizes that over a certain amount of time, the asset should increase in its value.

A feature of calls is how they involve an expiration date, which relies on the contract that an individual has entered into. The desired commodity could be purchased before the expiry date.

Puts Options Trading

Puts are also the absolute opposite of kind of alternatives for calls. A person who holds the put option seems to have the right to sell the underlying properties.

The sale method appears to have a negotiated price set for the potential act.

This situation occurs in capital markets during fascinating periods. If a person has predicted the worth of the assets will fall, she or he is easy to slip into motion. There are parallels among calls and puts, but the call is the opposite. A big common phenomenon is that both are restricted to the set period. Puts also have an expiry date for the contract that one has entered into.

American Type Options Trading

American type has little to do with the selling and buying of agreements as they filter down to choices. It sets eyes on the conditions laid out in an arrangement in the contractual language.

Simple information at this stage is that options come, including an expiry date in their deals, which allows a broker the ability to either purchase or sell an underlying commodity in the stock markets. A person has the opportunity, in the American type choice, to use her or his agreement before the contract expiry date. The said versatility appears to favor a trader by utilizing options in American type.

European Type Options Trading

Persons who are given this sort of choice do not have the same versatility as those who utilize American-style agreements are feeling. In this sort of alternative, the timetable is quite stringent. A person who uses contracts of a European type shall only exchange her or his fundamental properties on the expiry date and not after or before the expiry date.

Market-Traded Options Trading

It is also widely recognized by many stock market players as the listed options around the globe. It can be considered one of the most growing kinds of choices known to humans. Some choice contracts are listed in the markets for public trading. These are the types of stocks classified as market-traded shares. Also, with the assistance of delicate brokers, they can be sold or bought by anybody.

Over-Counter Options Trading

These trading options are often available in the counter-markets. These specific features combine over counter trading alternatives, making them not readily available to the public at large. Compared to certain types of exchange options, the details of contracts in such types of trading options appear to be complex.

Employee Shares Options Trading

This type of share options is well established to be offered to workers. This agreement can be issued to a worker of a given business proposing choice by the organization with which she or he is employed.

Its general purpose is to make the compensation package easy for the staff. It proceeds to work as compensation or benefits offered to workers of a particular company. This has many benefits as it encourages employees to work with these organizations.

Settled Cash Options Trading

These forms of agreement are not distinguished by the actual movement of the goods transferred. What occurs in a settled cash alternative may be correlated with the label it holds. Profits earned from this sort of alternative are paid to the top group in cash shapes.

There're several explanations for why this form of trading options occurs. It happens when the moved commodity becomes costly or difficult to be.

Expiry Based Options Trading Types

Agreements can be listed as per their dates of expiry. This applies to such anomalies where a seller is expected to be willing to offer inside a deal concerning the agreed date. The sources accepted that selling options continue to vary from the intervals they own. This involves as follows:

- **Options Trading Daily**

These are focused on the periods negotiated in exchange, as specified in the agreements. In an economical year, one is expected to also have four months of expiry to pick.

- **Options Trading Weekly**

They were launched in 2005 and are often referred to as the weeklies. We have the same values as standard choices, under which we felt they had that timing. Weeklies appear to be found in financial products with limitations.

- **Options Trading Quarterly**

Throughout the currency markets, they mentioned the expiry dates as near or identical to the finance divisions. Few individuals name them weeklies because, on the final day of delivery, they disappear.

Fundamental Security-Based Options Trading Types

A share option is a common one that has become the subject as people begin to address options for trading. That is where associated properties will be publicly reported as just a financial asset. Common awareness is for those who have been investing in this type of commerce. In this scenario, there are many kinds of choices involved. This involves as follows:

- **Stocks Options Trading**

A public owned business does have its stock are; these fundamental type assets exchanged throughout this deal.

- **Indexes Options Trading**

These seem to be similarly analogous to equity options. There is one distinction, though, which portrays the fuzzy thread. The break occurs when stocks are not the fundamental type of protection being bought and sold; instead. They 're indexes for a business.

- **Currencies Option Trading**

This arrangement does have a clear distinction from all other alternative types. This's because selling or purchasing money allows a dealer the opportunity. Trade is made at negotiated contract terms.

- **Forthcoming Options Trading**

In this type of trading, each future agreement is a fundamental asset. A forthcoming Options does have the power to offer an investor the opportunity to enter a future deal.

- **Assets Options Trading**

The element focused throughout this form of trading appears to just be a tangible product.

- **Baskets Options Trading**

It's just a type of options dealing which has as fundamental assets many financial products.

Exotic Trading Options Types

It is a term used to define those contract options that options traders have customized. The end outcome of this tailoring creates the agreements more complex. In certain instances, they are called non-standardized alternatives.

These are extra exotic agreements that are found only within the Cash market. Any of such options agreements, though, have begun to be popular in the new stock markets. This involves as follows:

- **Blockade Options Trading**

A wage-out shall also be rendered to the owners of such a type of agreement till such time because as price specified throughout this agreement hits.

- **Binary (Fixed) Options Trading**

In the case that the agreement ends, the holder of the financial statement's properties shall be granted a fixed sum of money.

- **Selective Options Trading**

These trading options enable a finance investor to select to either call or bring in at any moment.

- **Combined Options Trading**

One such option is a type of trade option wherein the financial statements asset.

CHAPTER 2:

Pros and Cons of Options

Pros of Trading Options

There is often confusion about why traders choose options when stocks and bonds do just fine. What some tend to miss out is the vast difference in the earnings potential. Stocks generally return a profit of 8% - 12% per annum, which is pretty impressive in and of itself. However, options are a lot more lucrative with a much larger potential.

Some options trades typically generate profits upwards of 50%. Making 100% profits within a short period of time and even more, is not unheard of. This is why a lot of experienced traders choose options. They are extremely lucrative and highly profitable. It is also possible to make money trading options in any market condition.

Traders can make money when the market is bullish, bearish, and even when it is stagnant. As such, you do not need specific market conditions, and hence profitability throughout the year is very possible.

Experts agree that trading options offer plenty of benefits that are not offered by other types of securities. While not all traders may want to engage in options trading, there are certain aspects of it that other traders find attractive.

Potential for Astronomical Profits

One of the main reasons for trading options is the opportunity of making significantly large profits compared to all other forms of trade in the markets. This is possible even without large sums of money. The principle behind this approach is leverage. A trader needs not to have large amounts of funds to earn huge profits. For instance, with as little as $10,000, it is possible to earn amounts such as $300,000 or even $800,000 simply by using leverage.

Take the example of a trader whose trading fund is $10,000. The trader wishes to invest this amount in Company ABC. Now the current stock price is $20 though this price is expected to rise. The trader could use the funds to directly purchase the shares and receive a total of 500 shares for his money. If the stock price was to rise to $25 within a month, the trader would have made $5 per share or a total of $2,500 in profits.

Alternatively, the trader could purchase call options of XYZ stocks with the same amount of money. The options allow the trader to purchase back the underlying stocks within a certain period of time. Now, options contracts cost between $1 and $4 depending on certain factors such as the value of the underlying security. In our example, one call options costs $2 so for the $10,000, the trader receives 5,000 options contracts. If the trader chooses to exercise the right to sell the underlying shares in the next month, then he stands to make a profit of $5 per share. Remember that he has a right to a total of 5,000 shares for a total profit of $25,000. This clearly demonstrates the capacity and power of options as well as how profitable this kind of trade can be.

Great Risk vs. Reward Consideration

Like all good traders, it is essential to weight the risk posed by a certain trade compared to the possible rewards. When trading using options, then the style adapted will indicate the type of risk inherent in the trade. The above example clearly shows how profitable options trading process is. If a loss was to be incurred in the above instance, then the total loss would have been the cost of the options.

In this instance, the risk is well worth the reward because the amount set to be lost is insignificant compared to the amount of profit to be made. In general, the higher the risk than the higher the potential return. Any time that a trader considers a trade, then the risk versus reward ratio should be taken into consideration.

As an options trader, you should learn how to benefit from volatility. Volatility needs to be your friend and partner as you can benefit from sharp and sudden movements in the markets. Options are mostly affected by implied volatility, which is essentially the most crucial factor affecting options prices. You need to learn to be on the lookout for implied volatility and determine whether it is low or high. This way, you will easily be able to get a sense of direction regarding the type of options to engage with.

Versatility and Flexibility

Another extremely appealing benefit of trading in options is the inherent flexibility. Options offer lots of flexibility with dozens of different strategies to pursue. This compares really well with numerous other trade and investment options out there. Most of these do not offer as much flexibility as options do. Also, most other securities have limited strategies, and this tends to limit the flexibility that a trader has on that security.

Take stocks, for instance. Even stock traders encounter certain limitations that are not inherent in options trading. There are plenty of strategies ranging from simple to compound to complex strategies. Stock traders generally buy, hold, or sell stocks. There isn't much else that they can do. This contrasts greatly with options because of the tens of strategies available to them. The versatility and flexibility inherent in options trading far surpass that of most other securities.

Firstly, options' flexibility allows them to be traded based on a wide variety of underlying securities. The variety and range of options strategies are massive. Also, the spreads provide real flexibility in the manner in which they can be traded. Traders have flexibility and versatility when it comes to limiting risks of assuming market positions when it comes to hedging, and even simply trying to benefit from stock movements, there are numerous opportunities available.

Cons of Options Trading

While options trading can be extremely profitable, it can also be extremely disastrous. This is why beginners need to stick to the basic strategies until they acquire sufficient knowledge, understanding, and experience. After a while, it will be possible to apply more advanced and even complex strategies that are very likely to make a profit regardless of market conditions. Risks remain, though, so it is always better to be cautious at the onset.

Traders must understand the risks and cons associated with trading options. The numerous benefits have seen more and more traders, including amateurs and pros, venture into the world of options in the hope of cashing in on this lucrative trade.

Are Options an Easy Task?

Options are securities. They are actually contracts that come with certain terms. These terms need to be clearly understood and taken into consideration at all times. Part of the options contracts has to do with time. Unlike stocks and other securities, options have a time limit. This time decay factor makes them extremely short-lived. If a trading strategy does not work out, then the options could expire worthlessly.

One of the most prohibitive factors about trading options is its complex nature. The basics are quite okay and relatively simple to comprehend. However, they have a limited scope as well as limited profitability. Real profitability lies in compounded strategies, which can be fit your business better once you gained advanced or proficient skills.

Traders can lose funds if they do not master options correctly. Learning how to trade options is possible, but it is a process that takes both commitment and time. Only traders who are dedicated and invest their time and effort will be rewarded with success.

Basically, all investment opportunities and even trading ventures carry a certain element of risk. The traders most at risk are beginners and novices. These groups are generally not as well versed or sufficiently experienced to deal with options. Knowledge is crucial in an options trade, but the experience is absolutely essential.

Yet the options trading process has been popularly utilized in the management of risks. Traders with stocks and other securities often buy options to protect themselves from inherent losses. Let us say a trader is holding stock ABC and predicts that its value will fall by 30% in the next one month. This trader has two options in this case. The first one is to sell the stock and hope to attract a great price. The other is to purchase a call option as a form of hedging against any market risks.

Even seasoned traders sometimes lose money. Chances of making huge profits exist, but the chances of losing large amounts also exist. It all depends on the strategies applied, a trader's experience, and amounts involved.

The best advice is to learn as much about trading options as possible and to understand the basics as clearly as possible. Plenty of practice also helps. Traders with little or no experience need to put their skills to practice as often as possible. There are plenty of platforms that provide dummy trading platforms where prospective traders can try out different strategies.

There are also plenty of tools and solutions that make options trading easier. All these, when applied to different strategies, can result in better performance at the markets. Once the basic strategies are well understood and practiced sufficiently, a trader can then proceed to implement and finesse them until the confidently execute them flawlessly. This is how a trader goes from beginner to novice, to advanced, and eventually professional trading levels.

This is why learning as much as possible about options can be really profitable. Plenty of excellent traders have seen their fortunes turn around by simply applying these strategies after taking months and sometimes years to perfect them.

CHAPTER 3:

Understand the Risks of Options Trading

The options trading process does carry some risks with it. Understanding these risks and taking mitigating steps will make you not just a better trader but a more profitable one as well. A lot of traders love options trading because of the immense leverage that this kind of trading affords them. Should an investment work out as desired, then the profits are often quite high. With stocks, you can expect returns of between 10%, 15%, or even 20%. However, when it comes to options, profit margins, more than 1,000% are very possible.

As an investor or trader, you should never spend more than 3% to 5% of your funds in any single trade. For instance, if you have $10,000 to invest, you should not spend more than $300 to $500 on any one trade.

Also, as a trader, you are not just mitigating against potential risks but are also looking to take advantage of the leverage. This is also known as gaining a professional trader's edge. While it is crucial to reduce the risk through careful analysis and selection of trades, you should also aim to make huge profits and enjoy big returns on your trades. There will always be some losses, and as a trader, you should get to appreciate this. However, your major goal as a trader should be to ensure that your wins are much, much larger than any losses that you may suffer.

All types of investment opportunities carry a certain level of risk. However, options trading carry a much higher risk of loss. Therefore, ensure that you have a thorough understanding of the risks and always be on the lookout. Also, these kinds of trades are very possible due to nature and leverage offered by options. A savvy trader realizes that he or she can control an almost equivalent number of shares as a traditional stock investor but at a fraction of the cost. Therefore, when you invest in options, you can spend a tiny amount of money to control a large number of shares. This kind of leverage limits your risks and exposure compared to a stock investor.

Time Is Not on Your Side

You need to keep in mind that all options have an expiration date and that they do expire in time. When you invest in stocks, time is on your side most of the time. However, things are different when it comes to options. Basically, the closer that an option gets to its expiration, the quicker it loses its value and earning potential.

Options deterioration is usually rather rapid, and it accelerates in the last days until expiration. Basically, as an investor, ensure that you only invest dollar amounts that you can afford to lose. The good news, though, is that there are a couple of actions that you can take to get things on your side.

- Trade mostly in options with expiration dates that are within the investment opportunity

- Buy options at or very near the money

- Sell options any time you think volatility is highly-priced

- Buy options when you are of the opinion that volatility is underpriced

Prices Can Move Pretty Fast

Options are highly leveraged financial instruments. Because of this, prices tend to move pretty fast. Basically, options prices can move huge amounts within minutes and sometimes even seconds. This is unlike other stock market instruments like stocks that move-in hours and days.

Small movements in the price of a stock can have huge implications on the value of the underlying stock. You need to be vigilant and monitor price movements often.

However, you can generate profits without monitoring activity on the markets twenty-four hours a day.

As an investor or trader, you should seek out opportunities where chances of earning a significant profit are immense. The opportunity should be sufficiently robust so that pricing by seconds will be of little concern. In short, search for opportunities that will lead to large profits even when you are not accurate when selling.

When structuring your options, you should ensure that you use the correct strike prices as well as expiration months to cut out most of the risk. You should also consider closing out your trades well before the expiration of options. This way, time value will not dramatically deteriorate.

Naked Short Positions Can Result in Substantial Losses

Anytime that your naked short option presents a high likelihood of substantial and sometimes even unlimited losses. Shorting put naked means selling stock options with no hedging of your position.

When selling a naked short, it simply implies that you are actually selling a call option or even a put option but without securing it using an option position, stock, or cash. It is advisable to sell a put or a call in combination with other options or with stocks. Remember that whenever you short sell a stock, you are, in essence, selling borrowed stock. Sooner or later, you will have to return the stock.

Fortunately, with options, there is no borrowing of stock or any other security.

CHAPTER 4:

Binary Options

Binary options are similar to traditional options in many ways except that they ultimately boil down to a basic yes or no question. Instead of worrying about what exact price an underlying stock is going to have, a binary option only cares if it is going to be above one price at the time of its expiration.

Traders then make their trades based on if they believe the answer is yes or no, at which time it will be worth either $0 or $100. While it may seem simple on its face, it is important that you fully understand how binary options work, as well as the time frames and markets they work with.

It is also important to understand the specific advantages and disadvantages that they have and which companies are legally allowed to offer binary options for trade.

They are also a great way for those who are interested in day-trading but don't have the serious capital required to get off the ground, to ply their trade. Traditional stock day trading limits don't apply with binary options, so you are allowed to start trading with just 1, $100 deposit. It is also important to keep in mind that binary options are a derivative created by its association with an underlying asset, which means they don't give you ownership of that asset in any way. As such, you would be unable to exercise them as a means of generating dividends or utilizing voting rights.

The Benefits of Picking Binary Options

The potential for a high return: this is a risky form of investing, but if you learn to read the market properly, you will find that it has a lot of potential for a lot of money to come to you. If you do well with this trading option, you could see a return on investment between 60 to 90 percent.

The risk is fixed: You will know right at the beginning how much money you stand to lose or to win depending on which way the prediction goes. This helps make it easier to decide on your choices. Other investments can end up being a lot of guesswork, and if things go south, you can lose a lot more than you put into the whole thing. On the other hand, with binary options, you know exactly how much you stand to gain and lose right off the top.

You can even win after losing: Since you will find that the risks on these options are high, some brokers offer a return on money that you invested if your predictions were wrong. This is not going to be the full amount but getting a small percentage of your money back can be encouraging compared to losing it all.

Easy trading: These are easier to trade on. Other options in the stock market make this hard, but the platforms for binary options help the investor trade without all the hassle. You can work with a live chat feature to do this or even with your broker if you have some questions. Besides, there are really only two options for most of your trading options, so this makes things easier as well.

Rewards: The risk associated with any binary option is always going to cap out at the cost of the initial trade because the worst result for any option is for it to time out and be worth $0. The reward is also capped and based on the amount of the initial investment. As an example, if you purchase a $20 binary option, then you are always going to make $100 at most, which means you will make $80 and have a 4:1 risk/reward ratio, which is better than you will find in most other situations most of the time.

This will only be in your benefit for a limited time, however, as gains will never increase pass $100 regardless of how much movement an underlying asset may have. The easiest way to mitigate this particular downside is to simply double down on options contracts from the start.

How to Trade Binary Options

Binary options are currently traded on the Nadex exchange, which was the first exchange created expressly to sell binary options in the United States. It offers market access as well as its own trading platform, which always has access to the most recent binary options pricing.

It is also possible to trade options on the Chicago Board Options Exchange, which can be accessed by those with an options trading approved brokerage account through more traditional means. When doing so, it is important to keep in mind that not all brokers are going to offer options trading, which means that if this is a route you are considering going down, you will need to plan accordingly and choose your broker with these services in mind.

Trading via Nadex costs 90 cents per trade with a maximum fee of $9 per transaction, which means that lots greater than 10 are essentially free.

The fee is not deducted from the trading account until the trade has expired, and if the trade does not end profitably, then there is no charge as well. Trading on the Chicago Board is subject to traditional brokerage fees.

Choosing the right market: Nothing is stopping you from trading across various asset classes at once when it comes to binary options and, indeed, Nadex allows trading across most of the major indices including the S&P 500, Nasdaq 100, Russell 2000 and the Dow 30. Available global indices include those from the UK, Germany, and Japan. Trades are also available for a variety of forex pairs, including AUD/JPY, EUR/GBP, USD/CHF, GBP/JPY, USD/CAD, AUD/USD, EUR/JPY, USD/JPY, GBP/UDS, and EUR/USD.

Another popular option through Nadex is the commodity binary options, which include crude oil, natural gas, gold, copper, silver, corn, and soybeans.

Binary option timeframes

Weekly trading

Weekly binary options are listings that provide the opportunity for trading in the short-term along with lots of opportunities to hedge the choices you do make. As you might infer from the name, weekly trading means working with options that expire in exactly one week, with the standard being for them to be listed on Thursday and expire the next Friday.

While this type of binary options trading has been around for quite some time, they were largely only used by investors who followed the cash indices. This exclusivity has changed in the past decade as the Chicago Board has started expanding the practice of this type of trading until now there are nearly 1,000 opportunities to do so each week.

Beyond just having a specific timeframe, weekly binary options are different than more traditional options in that they can only be purchased 21 days out of the month, which is why they aren't listed as expiring in the monthly style. As such, in the week that monthly options are set to expire, they are technically classified as weekly options.

The biggest benefit of this type of binary option is that it makes it extremely easier to purchase exactly what you are looking for in a specific trade without needing to come up with additional capital just to end up with more than you actually need. For those who are interested in selling, weekly binary options make it easier to do so more regularly as opposed to having to wait a month or more between sales. Weekly binary options trades are also worth considering in that they ultimately lead to lower costs for trades with larger spreads like calendar or diagonal spreads as you can sell weekly binary options against them in the interim.

They also come in handy when it comes to higher volumes of trades overall, especially when it comes to hedging larger positions in risky markets. Likewise, if the market is range-bound, the weekly market will still be fruitful thanks to strategies like the iron condor or iron butterfly.

The biggest downside to weekly binary options is that you won't have much of a chance of things changing in your favor if you choose poorly from the start. Likewise, if you are looking to short the binary option in question, then it is important to keep in mind that it would only take a relatively small overall move to push something into the money.

As you will have less time with which to turn a profit when dealing with weekly binary options when you do make a move it is vital that your timing is as precise as possible as if you choose poorly then you can easily find yourself paying for something that will end up being worthless practically as soon as you put your money down. It is also important to consider how much risk the option offers, as buying in bulk is always cheaper if you have the data to back it up.

Along similar lines, it is important to avoid naked puts or calls when trading in the weekly timeframe as these often end up with a lower probability of success overall. If you are quite specific when it comes to the directions of your chosen trades, then a structured trade or a debit spread may be a better choice.

Selling weekly at a reliable pace for the long-term can lead to reliable profits when done correctly. It is likely to only work out if you strive to define your profits from the start, which means you always need to know the odds on all of your current options to avoid selling yourself short by mistake. Selling weekly makes it easier to secure reliable profits while requiring extra margin to prevent unmitigated losses if you end up choosing poorly.

The most reliable type of trades to move forward within this scenario it is important to look into trades with lots of implied volatility as it is more likely to work out in your favor in the long run due to the either/or nature of binary options. Spreads are another useful way to make money from the weekly market as the overall implied volatility will typically be higher when compared to the monthly variation, which means the spread can help deal with an unexpected change in direction with speed required to do something about it. Selling against a long option, meanwhile, will serve to decrease the amount of volatility in the transaction, which means the ideal point to use the debit spread will be near the current price, assuming the ratio of risk to reward is close to 1 to 1.

Intraday trading

While binary options are typically not considered when it comes to a successful day trading strategy, this new trend is quickly gaining steam as traders realize that many of the standard day trading techniques can be used when it comes to buying and selling binary options successfully.

When it comes to day trading options, you will find some unique challenges that can be bested with proper planning. The first issue you will need to be on the lookout for is the fact that price movement tends to decrease in value more significantly thanks to the time value that is associated with options that are only near the money when they are close to expiring. It is also important to keep in mind that while their inherent value may increase, this may be countered by the loss incurred by the dropping time value.

CHAPTER 5:

When to Exit an Options Trade

Squaring off the options contract early when in profit, instead of waiting for a chance to exercise the option, makes a lot of sense — this is especially true for European style options in which the exercising of an option can be done only at the time of expiry.

Either way, irrespective of whether a given option follows the American or European style, it is far more prudent to square-off a trade, when in profit, rather than waiting till expiry to exercise the option and risk losing that profit (or even ending in a loss) in the event of a reversal in the direction of the underlying stock.

Note: After you enter an options trade, you exit that trade by squaring-off your position – this means if you are a buyer, you have to sell to close your position, and if you are a seller, you have to buy to close your position. However, at the time of expiry, if you haven't closed an open position, your position gets squared-off automatically based on the price of the underlying stock/index.

Meanwhile, let's get back to our old friend Bob and his Call option trade to illustrate the point pointed out earlier.

We know what happened after Bob bought a call option from Jacob - the market price for a cow eventually rose to $2,500 from the original

$2,000 and Bob exercised his option, claimed his cows, and sold them off at the market price, thereby closing his trade for a handsome profit.

If this particular example was an actual stock market trade and if Bob was dealing with a stock market option, then Bob would have had the ability to exercise his option before the expiry date only if his options contract followed the American style of expiry.

If Bob had an options contract that could only be exercised at the time of expiry (European style), and his position was already in profits well before the expiry date, he would not have ideally waited till the expiry date to book his profit. He would have booked a profit much earlier by selling off the options contract itself.

If you remember correctly when Bob bought the option from Jacob, he paid a premium of $50 for the option (the overall contract amount was $250 since it covered 5 cows), and Bob's contract entitled him to buy Jacob's cows at $2,000 each. At that time, the market price for a cow was also $2,000.

Therefore, in options terminology, we can say the market price of the stock was equal to the strike price of the option when Bob bought his option, or in other words, that particular option was an ATM option.

The last statement also implies that Bob's option had no intrinsic value at the time of purchase. If the market price for a cow hadn't appreciated and had remained at $2,000 for the duration of the contract validity, this option's premium value of $50 would have eroded each day, and the option would have eventually expired worthless. Nevertheless, the premium of that option was $50 to begin with, because it had one full month remaining for expiry, and therefore, time-value.

In an alternate scenario, let us assume that 10 days after Bob's contract with Jacob was in place, Bob saw that cow prices had already touched $2,300. Since he had 20 more days remaining for expiry, Bob decides he doesn't want to wait till the expiry date, and he would rather book a profit immediately by selling the call option itself to a third-party.

Bob bought the option for $50 at a strike price of $2,000 when the market price of the cow was $2,000. But when the market price for a cow went up to $2,300, the value of the call option itself owned by Bob would also have accordingly risen to about $310.

A rise from $50 to $310 is a rather steep climb up, isn't it?

Did you understand why the premium for Bob's option went up from $50 to $310 when the market price of a cow went up from $2,000 to $2,300?

It's not that complicated, actually.

The option premium shot up because it is now deep in-the-money (ITM), and it has an intrinsic value of $300 already (the remaining $10 is time-value). In contrast, at the time the option was purchased, it was an ATM option and had no intrinsic value but only a time-value of $50.

Previously when the market price of the cow was only $2,000, if Bob had exercised his contract, he would not have made any profit - he'd practically have to buy a cow at $2,000 (strike-price) and sell it at $2,000 (market-price) were he to exercise his option immediately. However, when the market price of the cow went up to $2,300, Bob's contract entitled him to purchase Jacob's cows at the old price of $2,000. Therefore, that contract's intrinsic value became $300 – in other words, exercising that option now would yield a profit of $300 (The market price of $2,300 minus the Strike-price of $2,000).

With 20 days left before the expiry of the contract, there would also be some associated time premium (approximated to $10 in this case). Therefore, the value of one single call option contract would have jumped to $310 or so from the original $50. Therefore, Bob just needed to sell that options contract to another trader at the current value of $310 to bag a profit of $260 on each cow which is covered by the contract ($260 = the current premium value of that call option, $310, minus the premium originally paid, $50). Bob's overall profit, therefore, would then be $260 x 5 (no. of cows covered as part of that contract) = $1300. Bob will make a neat profit and the new owner of the options contract Bob originally purchased from Jacob will now have to wait till the time of expiry to exercise that option or alternately, he/she too can sell the contract itself to a fourth person, if a suitable opportunity presents itself. Having the discipline to sell off a contract when it becomes profitable is important because if you hold on to it for too long, there is a possibility the tide may turn. You may end up losing a portion of your profits or may even end in a loss. Plus, if you are a buyer, then the advantage of selling an option as early as possible will ensure you retain maximum time premium, which would otherwise keep eroding every day as the option approaches expiry. **Note 1:** All options have an associated time-value and an intrinsic value - while the former is dependent on how far the option is from its expiry date and becomes zero at expiry, the latter is applicable only for ITM options and would be equal to the difference between the strike price of that option and the market price of the underlying.

Note 2: While the example above had mentioned that the premium of the option went from $50 to $310 when the price of a cow went up, the premium amount of $310 was an approximated amount for the sake of general understanding. In reality, the actual amount of appreciation in the premium could vary depending on the various factors that affect the options pricing at that time.

CHAPTER 6:

Technical Analysis and Its Benefits

Technical analysis is a strategy of trading where investments and trading opportunities evaluation and identification are taken up by analysis of the trending statistics of the trade in the market.

The analysts focus on how price movement and the volume of stocks affect the business to know the entry and the exit.

The analysis's main focus is on the patterns of the progress of prices, the signals in the trade that tells the trader to enter or exit, the charting tools, and how they work. Realization of strength or weakness of securities is a primary focus for the trader

This analysis helps the trade know the entry and exit time.

Charles Dow in the 1800s coined this analysis. After Charles coming up with the Dow Theory, other researchers like William P, Robert, Hamilton Edson, and John gave their ideas that helped form a strong basis of the theory. Technical analyses continued evolving and took encompassed different patterns and signals throughout the years of research. The analysts in technical analysis believe that the history of a security's price swings is of much significance for it predicts the future price of the security. Technical analysis assumes that the price of security alone shows the public information of the security, and therefore, its importance is to follow up on the price movement.

While using technical analysis, you need to use the right approach to be able to understand the trade well. There are two different approaches to technical analysis, and these are the top-down technique and the bottom-up technique.

Top-Down Technique

This technique mostly applies to short term trades. The trend analysis starts from the longtime frames then they come down to the short time frame. The analysts here asses the economy globally before assessing the significant scale trends in the economies.

They determine the big scale trends within the economies which they think have the best investment opportunities. The analysts here always starts on a broader scale before narrowing down to what they believe as opportunities. They then evaluate the sectors that can take advantage of the trends of the security in the market. Then they finally select the underlying assets in the sectors that are favorable.

Bottom-Up Technique

This method of analysis applies mostly in long time trades. The investors here analyze the trade by looking at different companies individually and then create a business of the company on the market basing on the company's characteristics. Most investors here are small scale investors.

They look at specific attributes of a company when building the portfolio for it. They mostly buy and hold for a long time while researching the markets to get the appropriate time to see. Despite the delay in releasing their held stocks, the risk of loss is low, and the return over the period or the risk-adjusted returns go up.

Different traders also prefer using separate technical analysis. For instance, day traders mostly prefer trend lines and volume indicators. These help them make decisions about their entry and exit in the trade. On the other hand, the swing traders select the chart patterns and the technical indicators in their analysis. There is another group of investors, the developers of algorithms. These types of traders prefer using both the volume indicators and the technical indicators in their analysis to help them come up with decisions about the trade.

Support and resistance levels analysis helps a trader know when to enter or exit. A support level is reached when prices are expected to take an upward trend after touching the support line. While the resistance level is when the prices are expected to go down after reaching the resistance level. Investors should be keen when analyzing the support and resistance levels in any trade.

When a resistance level is hit, a sell signal is set off. The prices are not likely to go past this level. Traders should sell their securities at this level because eventually, the prices will start falling, which will give them losses if they still hold on their securities. However, when the prices move past the support and resistance level, the work of the levels becomes reversed. The new level reached by support level price breakthrough below it becomes the new resistance level. While when the price breakthrough above the support level, then the resistance level reached becomes the new support level. Support and resistance technical analysis method is essential in all trades. It helps the trader be on the right track of the market and know when to buy or sell to remain in the business.

Characteristics of Technical Analysis

- Technical analysis looks at the historical market data of securities that includes the price movement of the security in the market and the volume of the trading.

- Technical analysis believes that the data acquired from the market is sufficient enough for the market itself is an indicator of the future prices and trends of the security. The analysis believes that the market price is a predictor.

- Studies the patterns of security through mathematical analysis tools like trend lines, charts, support and resistance, and many others.

- Believes chart patterns are likely to repeat themselves.

- Technical analysis studies the movement in the market and not the goods in the market.

- It believes that the market is never wrong.

- Technical analysis answers the question of what you should trade.

When working with technical analysis, you are always going to want to remember that it functions because of the belief that the way the price of a given trade has moved in the past is going to be an equally reliable metric for determining what it is likely to do again in the future.

Regardless of which market you choose to focus on, you'll find that there is always more technical data available than you will ever be able to realistically parse without quite a significant amount of help.

Luckily, you won't be sifting through the data all on your own, and you will have numerous technical tools, including things such as charts, trends, and indicators to help you push your success rates to new heights.

While some of the methods you will be asked to apply might seem arcane at first, the fact of the matter is that all you are essentially doing is looking to determine future trends along with their relative strengths.

This, in turn, is crucial to your long-term success and will make each of your trades more reliable practically every single time.

Understand core assumptions: Technical analysis is all about measuring the relative value of a particular trade or underlying asset by using available tools to find otherwise invisible patterns that, ideally, few other people have currently noticed.

When it comes to using technical analysis properly, you are going to always need to assume three things are true. First and foremost, the market ultimately discounts everything; second, trends will always be an adequate predictor of price, and third, history is bound to repeat itself when given enough time to do so.

Technical analysis believes that the current price of the underlying asset in question is the only metric that matters when it comes to looking into the current state of things outside of the market, specifically because everything else is already automatically factored in when the current price is set as it is.

As such, to accurately use this type of analysis, all you need to know is the current price of the potential trade-in question as well as the greater economic climate as a whole.

Those who practice technical analysis are then able to interpret what the price is suggesting about market sentiment to make predictions about where the price of a given cryptocurrency is going to go in the future.

This is possible since pricing movements aren't random. Instead, they follow trends that appear in both the short and the long-term.

Determining these trends in advance is key to using technical analysis successfully because all trends are likely to repeat themselves over time, thus the use of historical charts to determine likely trends in the future.

When it comes to technical analysis, what is always going to be more important than the why?

That is, the fact that the price moved in a specific way is far more important to a technical analyst then why it made that particular movement.

Supply and demand should always be consulted, but beyond that, there are likely too many variables to make it worthwhile to consider all of them as opposed to their results.

The Benefits of Technical Analysis in Options Trading

There are a variety of benefits that you enjoy when you use technical analysis in trading options. The benefits arise from the fact that traders are usually asking a lot of questions touching on the price of the market and entry points. While the forecast for prices is a huge task, the use of technical analysis makes it easier to handle.

The major advantages of technical analysis include:

Expert Trend Analysis

This is the biggest advantage of technical analysis in any market. With this method, you can predict the direction of the market at any time. You can determine whether the market will move up, down, or sideways easily.

Entry and Exit Points

As a trader, you need to know when to place a trade and when to opt-out. The entry point is all about knowing the right time to enter the trade for good returns. Exiting a trade is also vital because it allows you to reduce losses.

Leverage Early Signals

Every trader looks for ways to get early signals to assist them in making decisions. Technical analysis gives you signals to trigger a decision on your part. This is usually ideal when you suspect that a trend will reverse soon. Remember the time the trend reverses are when you need to make crucial decisions.

It Is Quick

In options trading, you need to go with techniques that give you fast results. Additionally, getting technical analysis data is cheaper than other techniques in fundamental analysis, with some companies offering free charting programs. If you are in the market to make use of short time intervals such as 1-minute, 5-minute, 30 minute, or 1-hour charts, you can get this using technical analysis.

It Gives You a Lot of Information

Technical analysis gives you a lot of information that you can use to make trading decisions. You can easily build a position depending on the information you get then take or exit trades. You have access to information such as chart patterns, trends, support, resistance, market momentum, and other information.

The current price of an asset usually reflects every known information of an asset. While the market might be rife with rumors that the prices might surge or plummet, the current price represents the final point for all information.

As the traders and investors change their bearing from one part to another, the changes in assets reflect the current value perception.

If all this turns out to be true, then the only info you require is a price chart that gives all the price reflections and predictions. There isn't any need for you to worry yourself with the reasons why the price is rising or falling when you can use a chart to determine everything.

With the right technical analysis information, you can make trading easier and faster because you make decisions based not on hearsay but facts.

You don't have to spend your time reading and trying to make headway in financial news. All you need us to check what the chart tells you.

You Understand Trends

If the prices on the market were to gyrate randomly without any direction, you would find it hard to make money. While these trends run in all directions, the prices always move in trends.

Directional bias allows you to leverage the benefits of making money. Technical analysis allows you to determine when a trend occurs and when it doesn't occur, or when it is in reversal.

Many of the profitable techniques that are used by the traders to make money follow trends. This means that you find the right trend and then look for opportunities that allow you to enter the market in the same direction as the trend. This helps you to capitalize on the price movement.

Trends run in various degrees. The degree of the trend determines how much money you make, whether in the short term or long-term trading. Technical analysis gives you all the tools that make it possible for you to do this.

History Always Repeats Itself

Technical analysis uses common patterns to give you the information to trade. However, you need to understand that history will not be exact when it repeats itself, though.

The current analysis will be either bigger or smaller, depending on the existing market conditions. The only thing is that it won't be a replica of the prior pattern.

This pans out easily because most human psychology doesn't change so much, and you will see that the emotions have a hand in making sure that prices rise and fall.

The emotions that traders exhibit create a lot of patterns that lead to changes in prices all the time. As a trader, you need to identify these patterns and then use them for trading. Use prior history to guide you and then the current price as a trigger of the trade.

Enjoy Proper Timing

Do you know that without proper timing, you will not be able to make money at all? One of the major advantages of technical analysis is that you get the chance to time the trades. Using technical analysis, you get to wait, then place your money in other opportunities until it is the right time to place a trade.

Applicable Over a Wide Time Frame

When you learn technical analysis, you get to apply it to many areas in different markets, including options. All the trading in a market is based mostly on the patters that are a result of human behavior. These patterns can then be mapped out on a chart to be used across the markets. While there is some difference between analyzing different securities, you will be able to use technical analysis in most of the markets. Additionally, you can use the analysis in any timeframe, which is applicable whether you use hourly, daily, or weekly charts. These markets are usually taken to be fractal, which essentially means that patterns that appear on a small scale will also be present on a large scale as well.

Technical Analysis Secrets to Become the Best Trader

To make use of technical analysis the right way, you need to follow time-testing approaches that have made the technique a gold mine for many traders. Let us look at the various tips that will take you from novice to pro in just a few days:

Use More than One Indicator

Numbers make trading easy, but it also applies to the way you apply your techniques. For one, you need to know that just because one technical indicator is better than using one, applying a second indicator is better than using just one. The use of more than one indicator is one of the best ways to confirm a trend. It also increases the odds of being right.

As a trader, you will never be 100 percent right at all times, and you might even find that the odds are stashed against you when everything is plain to see. However, don't demand too much from your indicators such that you end up with analysis paralysis.

To achieve this, make use of indicators that complement each other rather than the ones that clash against each other.

Go for Multiple Time Frames

Using the same buy signal every day allows you to have confidence that the indicator is giving you all you need to know to trade. However, make sure you look for a way to use multiple timeframes to confirm a trend. When you have a doubt, it is wise that you increase the timeframe from an hour to a day or from a daily chart to a weekly chart.

Understand that No Indicator Measures Everything

You need to know that indicators are supposed to show how strong a trend is; they won't tell you much more. So, you need to understand and focus on what the indicator is supposed to communicate instead of working with assumptions.

Go with the Trend

If you notice that an option is trading upward, then go ahead and buy it. Conversely, when the trend stops trending, then it is time to sell it. If you aren't sure of what is going on in the market at that time, then don't make a move. However, waiting might make you lose profitable trades as opposed to trading. You also miss out on opportunities to create more capital.

Have the Right Skills

It really takes superior analytical capabilities and real skill to be successful at trading, just like any other endeavor. Many people think that it is hard to make money with options trading, but with the right approach, you can make extraordinary profits. You need to learn and understand the various skills so that you know what the market seeks from you and how to achieve your goals.

Trade with a Purpose

Many traders go into options trading with the main aim of having a hobby. Well, this way you won't be able to make any money at all. What you need to do is to trade for the money – strive to make profits unlike those who try to make money as a hobby.

Always Opt for High value

Well, no one tells you to trade any security that comes your way — it is purely a matter of choice. Try and go for high-value options so that you can trade them the right way. Make use of fundamental analysis to choose the best options to trade-in.

Be Disciplined

When using technical analysis, you might find yourself in situations that require you to make a decision fast. To achieve success, you need to have strict risk management protocols. Don't base on your track record to come up with choices; instead, make sure you follow what the analysis tells you.

Don't Overlook Your Trading Plan

The trading plan is in place to guide you when things go awry. Coming up with the plan is easy, but many people find it hard to implement the plan the right way. The trading plan has various components — the signals and the take-profit/stop-loss rules. Once you get into the market, you need to control yourself because you have already taken a leap. Remember, you cannot control the indicators once they start running — all you can do is to prevent yourself from messing up everything. Come up with the trading rules when you are unemotional to try and mitigate the effects of making bad decisions.

Accept Losses

Many people trade with one thing in mind — losses aren't part of their plan. This is a huge mistake because you need to understand that every trade has two sides to it — a loss and a profit. Remember that the biggest mistake that leads to losses isn't anything to do with bad indicators rather using them the wrong way. Always have a stop-loss order when you trade to prevent loss of money.

Have a Target When You Trade

So, what do you plan to achieve today? Remember, trading is a way to grow your capital as opposed to saving. Options trading is a business that has probable outcomes that you get to estimate. When you make a profit, make sure you take some money from the table and then put it in a safe place.

Price Charts

Technical analysis is all about the price chart, which is a chart with an x and y-axis. The price is measured along the vertical axis, and the time is measured via the horizontal axis. There are numerous different types of price charts that different types of traders prefer. These include the point and figure chart, the Renko chart, the Kagi chart, the Heikin-Ashi chart, the bar chart, the candlestick chart, the line chart, and the tick chart. However, the ones you will need to concern yourself with at first are going to be included in any forex trading platform software and are the bar chart, the candlestick chart, the line chart, and the point and click the chart, which is why they are outlined in greater detail below.

Line chart

Of all the various types of charts, the line charts are the simplest because it only presents price information in the form of closing prices in a fixed period. The lines that give it its name are created when the various closing price points are then connected with a line. When looking at a line chart, it is important to keep in mind that they will not be able to provide an accurate visual representation of the range that individual points reached, which means you won't be able to see either opening prices or those that were high or low before close. Regardless, the closing point is important to always consider, which is why this chart is so commonly referred to by technical traders of all skill levels.

Bar chart

A bar chart takes the information that can be found in a line chart and expands upon it in some interesting ways. For starters, the chart is made using some vertical lines that provide information on various data points. The top and bottom of the line can then be thought of as the high and low of the trading timeframe, respectively, while the closing price is also indicated with a dash on the right side of the bar. Furthermore, the point where the currency price opened is indicated via a dash and will show up on the left side of the bar in question.

Candlestick chart

A candlestick chart is similar to a bar chart, though the information it provides is much more detailed overall. Like a bar chart, it includes a line to indicate the range for the day. However, when you are looking at a candlestick chart, you will notice a wide bar near the vertical line, which indicates the degree of the difference the price saw throughout the day. If the price that the stock is trading at increases overall for the day, then the candlestick will often be clear, while if the price has decreased, then the candlestick is going to be read.

Point and figure chart

While seen less frequently than some of the other types of charts, a point and figure chart has been around for nearly a century and can still be useful in certain situations today. This chart can accurately reflect the way the price is going to move, though it won't indicate timing or volume. It can be thought of as a pure indicator of price with the excessive noise surrounding the market muted, ensuring nothing is skewed.

A point and figure chart are noticeable because it is made up of Xs and Os rather than lines and points. The Xs will indicate points where positive trends occurred while the Os will indicate periods of downward movement. You will also notice numbers and letters listed along the bottom of the chart, which corresponds to months as well as dates. This type of chart will also make it clear how much the price is going to have to move for an X to become an O or an O to become an X.

Trend or range

When it comes to using technical analysis successfully, you will want to determine early on if you are more interested in trading based on the trends you find or on the range. While they are both properties related to price, these two concepts are very different in practice, which means you will want to choose one to emphasize over the other. If you decide to trade according to trend, then you are more interested in going with the flow and choosing stocks to trade while everyone else is having the same idea.

Chart Patterns to Be Aware Of

Flags and Pennants

Both flags and pennants show retracement, which is deviations that will be visible in the short term concerning the primary trend. Retracement results in no breakout occurring from either the resistance or support levels, but this won't matter as the security will also not be following the dominant trend. The lack of breakout means this trend will be relatively short term.

The resistance and support lines of the pennant occur within a larger trend and converge so precisely that they practically form a point. A flag is essentially the same except that the resistance and support lines from the flag will be essentially parallel instead.

If you are looking for them, both flags and pennants are more likely to be found in the mid-section of the primary phase of the trend. They can last up to two weeks before being absorbed back into the primary trend line.

They are typically associated with falling volume, which means that if you notice a flag or a pennant and the volume is not falling, then you are more likely actually seeing a reversal, which is an actually changing trend instead of a simple retracement.

Head Above Shoulders Formation

If you are looking for indicators of how long any one particular trend is likely to continue, then looking for a grouping of three peaks in a price chart, known as the head above shoulders formation, can indicate a bearish pattern moving forward. The peaks to the left and to the right of the primary peak, also known as the shoulders, should be somewhat smaller than the head peak and also connect at a specific price. This price is known as the neckline, and when it reaches the right shoulder, the price will likely then plunge noticeably.

How to Apply Technical Analysis

Many traders have heard of technical analysis, but they don't know how to use it to make deductions and come up with decisions that impact their trades. Here are the different steps to make sure you have the right decision when you use technical analysis.

1. Identify a Trend

You need to identify an option and then see whether there is a trend or not. The trend might be driving the options up or down. The market is bullish if it is moving up and bearish when it is moving down.

As a trader, you need to go along with the trend instead of fighting it. When you fight against the trend, you incur unnecessary losses that will make it hard to achieve the rewards that you seek.

You also need to have good ways to identify the trend; this is because the market can move in a certain direction. It is not all about identifying the direction of the trend but also when the trend is moving out of the trend.

So, how can you identify a trend the right way? Here are some tools to use to get the right trend:

- Using triangles that map major swings
- Use the moving average
- Trend lines give you an idea of the direction of the trend

Once you identify the trend, the next step is to try and mark the support and resistance levels

2. Support and Resistance Levels

You need to understand the support and resistance levels that are within the trend. Use the Fibonacci retracement tool to identify these spots on the trend.

3. Look for Patterns

Patterns need to show you what to expect in a certain market. You can use candlesticks to determine the chart pattern.

Trend Indicators

Some indicators show you the strength and direction of the current market trend. Understand that despite their ability to do this, all signs are lagging. In other words, every single one of them tells you what has just happened.

They do not tell you what will happen. In addition to this, they also show you what happened with a bit of a delay built-in. This is understandable since they're two levels removed from the order flow. Hence, I do advise caution when it comes to building strategies around them for the long term.

The reason for this is that you'll miss a lot of opportunities over the long term. Think of it as making 1% less than the pure price chart trader per trade. Over a few trades, the done-for-you approach that indicator traders like might be worth it. However, if you consider a two-year period where you might place close to 500 trades, you'll end up 500% behind the other trader. That amount is no joke.

Having said that, indicators do hasten the learning process along nicely. So use them to learn about order flow balance while keeping in mind that you will need to move on eventually. As final proof of my words, let me say that you will not find professional traders at banks, hedge funds, or prop shops using an indicator based system. Every single one of them looks at the price chart directly, and indicators are used merely for support or to simplify complex things once in a while.

Let's dive into trend indicators now.

Moving Average Crossovers

A moving average line is simply the plot of the last n bars of price, laid over the price chart. For example, the 20 bar moving average is the graph of the previous twenty bars' closing prices, plotted as a curve. There are two kinds of moving averages, exponential and simple (ema and sma).

The ema is a more sensitive line and reacts to the price more while the sma is a smoother curve. Generally speaking, the lower your time frame, the more useful the sma will be. However, this isn't a deal-breaker. The high rate of its usage means that the 20 ema acts as a pretty good indicator of what the market is doing. A lot of professional traders use a break of the 20 ema as a sign of intermediate trend change.

With that said, this is not the way to use the 20 ema. Instead, it is best used in a crossover trading system. The crossover strategy aims to detect trend changes in price by having a faster ema crossover a slower ema. Faster and slower here refer to the time period of the averages.

Common combinations for a crossover are 5 and 20 or 15 and 45. So the 5 ema will be the faster average while the 20 ema will be the slower one. The idea is that the faster average will be a lot more sensitive to the changes in trend, and if it crosses above or below the slower ema, then it's a good bet that the trend is changing. Let's look at an example.

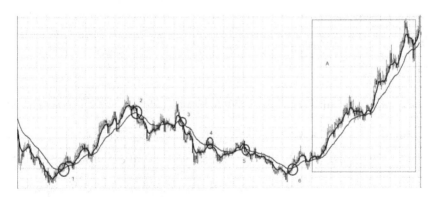

EMA Crossovers

In figure 8, the thick line indicates the 5 ema, while the thinner line indicates the 20 ema. Notice how the 5 ema tracks price movement closer than the 20 ema? Well, this is what the crossover strategy is all about. The places where you could have made a profit using this strategy are indicated by the circles, labeled 1 through 6.

Note that I haven't labeled a few crossovers that would have resulted in a loss. Either way, only a couple of them would have had this result, and in the long run, they don't matter much. You can see that this combination of emas predicts very short term trend changes quite well.

If you wish to predict longer-term trend changes, then increase the interval of the moving averages. There is a trade-off when doing this, of course. You won't be able to capture smaller movements. The key is to find a good balance and determine the right level of the interval you wish to trade.

One last thing in figure 8. Notice that when the trend really gets going as indicated in box A, the crossover strategy doesn't generate any signals. This is because the trend is too strong. This is a noted weakness of the crossover strategy. It won't help you enter strong trends once they've already begun. However, it will help you get in on the action before it begins.

If you were to blindly follow a crossover system without the help of reading s/r and order flow balance, you would be leaving a lot of money on the table in the long term. Taking figure 8 as an example, you would have determined beforehand that trend is bearish and, therefore, would have looked at the short side of the market.

This would have caused you to ignore signal 1, and you might have ignored a few of the ones between 3 and 5 as well since the price is in a range here. However, signal 6 would have alerted you to the fact that the trend might be changing. As price grows stronger, you would have started looking for bullish entries.

Thus, the crossover doesn't indicate an entry strategy, but the fact that tide has changed and that you should seek to enter as soon as possible. Once you do this, you would have ended up riding that huge uptrend inbox A, which would have more than made up for the few missed trades you would have otherwise taken in a blind crossover strategy.

In a nutshell, this illustrates the difference between accomplished traders and beginners. The successful traders look to get in on the big moves. Beginners are far more concerned about the number of entries they receive. Hence, look to make this switch as soon as possible.

Average Directional Movement- ADX

Crossovers are the most profitable trend indicator strategy precisely because they're so simple to implement. There are other indicators you can use, such as the ADX, which will give you the strength of the trend, but using them as a strategy is suspect because they're either too complicated or everyone else uses them.

ADX is a good indicator of the strength of the trend. Any value prints over 20 is a good sign of a strong trend. Anything over 30 is an extremely strong trend. There are no specific entry signals it provides by itself. You should simply use it as a reference when deciding on your bias in the market.

Note that the AD doesn't give you the trend direction but merely the strength. It can have an upward curve, even in bearish markets. You will often see two additional lines, the +DI and -DI within the ADX window. There are strategies you can design using them, but it's best to keep things simple with the ema crossovers and practice proper risk management to make money.

Momentum Oscillators

In contrast to trend indicators, oscillators seek to capture the momentum within a move. Given that the market is most often in a middling trend of sorts, with active counter-trend participation, it makes sense that oscillators are quite useful. Oscillators are best combined with other trend indicators, such as the ADX.

A profitable strategy is to look at the ADS and determine the strength of the trend. If it happens to be too strong, then the oscillator can be ignored. This highlights a weakness that all oscillators have, as we'll shortly see. When talking of oscillators, there are two that are evergreen, and both of them function in largely the same manner. These are the stochastic oscillator and the relative strength index or RSI.

Let's look at the stochastic first since this also incorporates a trading entry signal within it.

Stochastic Oscillator

Like all oscillators, the stochastic fluctuates in a bounded range between 0-100. The 0-20 is labeled the oversold level, and 80-100 is the overbought level. The idea behind these levels is that once price moves into them, it indicates that either demand or supply has become too much, and therefore, a reversal is due.

Thus, when price moves into the oversold level, you can expect a move back upwards. When it moves into the overbought level, you can expect a move downwards.

The only exception to this is during very strong trends. During these times, you can expect to see price hang around at these extreme levels for quite a long time without making any move in the opposite direction.

You need to, therefore, filter the stochastic signals with a trend indicator like the ADX to ensure that trend strength levels are appropriate. Anything below 40 is usually a good area to start looking at the stochastic seriously.

This won't hold for every stock there is, so you should look at individual stocks to determine their behavior. The stochastic itself consists of two lines called the signal and the main lines.

An entry signal is generated when the signal line crosses the mainline within the extreme zones of 0-20 and 80-100. Besides, the direction of the crossover determines the entry direction. So, if the signal crosses the mainline from below, you need to go long. Similarly, a crossover from above to below indicates a short position entry.

One last thing you could use to further filter entries is to wait for the mainline to leave the extreme zones. This does reduce profit a bit, but it helps you avoid a few losses, so the results average out over time. Figure 9 illustrates this strategy in action.

Figure 9- Stochastic Oscillator

The two horizontal lines within the stochastic window indicate the overbought and oversold zones, with the overbought one being on top. The circles indicate entry points, and the arrows on the price chart correspond roughly to the bars you ought would be entering on, depending on whether you wait for the price to leave the extreme zones or not. As you can see, not all the signals are profitable, but overall, they average out. Given that the price movement is tilted upwards but not very much so, this is an excellent performance. So how would you look at trading options with this?

Well, in such environments, you need to either adopt a long view or a very short view. The short view would involve you simply looking to capture the changes in premiums as opposed to letting your options expire with whatever premium levels they have. The long view would be you holding on for a month or so looking to capture the full value of the trade. For example, if you use the stochastic to enter long at the first arrow in figure 9, you would have seen that bearish representation is low and, therefore, a call spread would have worked well. You will need to keep adjusting the short call's level, and this will involve you covering the position quite a bit, but given the subsequent presence of bears, this level could have been brought a lot closer.

You will need to play around with these levels on demo and see what suits you best. There is no way for me to give you an exact playbook I'm afraid. You will need to do the hard work of learning the skill of identifying market conditions via order flow balance and then decide for yourself which levels to target with your options.

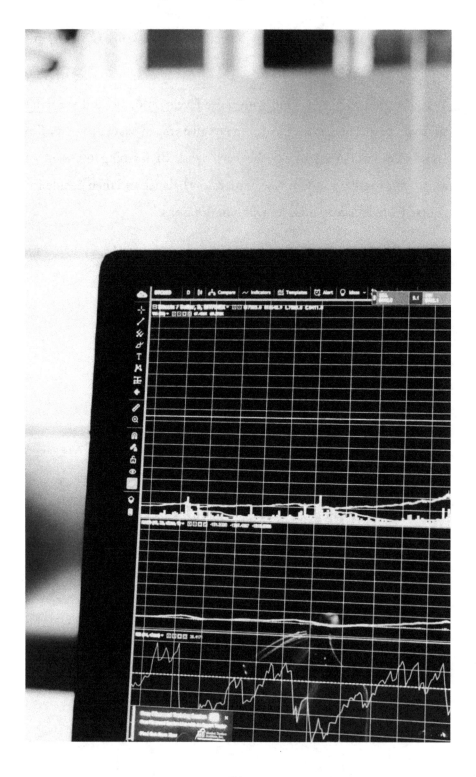

Conclusion

You can start trading options by only spending a few hundred dollars. This means you can take small risks and build up your account gradually. Even the best traders experience losses, it is part of the business. But, if you proceed strategically, you will learn how to trade effectively, and you can rack up much more wins than losses.

The best suggestion is to get started with some calls and puts on index funds. Start small, do not force the time, let your account grow, and be comfortable during your constant growth.

If you play your cards right, really study the market and make sound decisions – you will feel confident and proud of your profits.

So that's it! It's time to follow all steps. Again, thank you for choosing this book to teach you the basic principles of how to trade.

Options Trading Terminology

At the money: This term is used to describe the nearest price to the equity price during a particular trading moment.

Bearish: This term, on the other hand, describes a trader who believes that the market prices will do lower or the market will experience a downfall at particular trading activity in a specific period.

Bid spread: This is the actual difference between the asking price and the bid price for a given option during a particular options trading period.

Big chicken trade: This is a term used to describe a series of bull call calendars, and the bear put calendars.

Break-even point: This is the specific price that an underlying asset must reach to avoid the option buyer from acquiring losses if at all, they decided to exercise the option.

Bullish: This term is particularly referring to an investor who believes that a specific stock price will go higher or simply the market will rise higher.

Call option: This is an equity agreement that awards a buyer the chance to purchase 100 particular shares at a particular strike price within a specified time. A seller is also needed to sell off the stock at a particular price if the option gets exercised.

Credit: It is any value amount received in a particular trading account from the financial benefits experienced in various options trading activities. The profits and multiple benefits feed the trading accounts.

Commission: This is the fee charged in an options trading market after option orders have been executed on a securities exchange.

Contract: This is an agreement set between a buyer trader and a seller trader during a particular options trading activity.

Credit: It is any value amount received in a particular trading account from the financial benefits experienced in various options trading activities. The profits and multiple benefits feed the trading accounts.

Debit: This is any amount of cash paid out to purchase an option during a particular trading period.

Dip in the money: This is a term used to refer to multiple in-the-money occurrences that have been experienced in a particular trading period in the options market.

Downside risk: This is the estimation of a particular downfall market price that is likely to be experienced by the market during the end of a particular trading period.

Equity option: It is a kind of option that gives the owner, who happens to be the buyer, the chance to purchase and sell any available stock in the trading market at a specific share during a particular period before the expiration date is reached.

Ex-dividend: This is the actual date in which the stock enters the options trading market with the absence of dividends.

Expiry date: This is the actual date—day, month, or year—to which a particular options trading contract becomes invalid and null.

Front-month: When the expiration of two months is involved in options trading, the month nearer in time is normally considered.

Historical volatility: This is analyzing the actual volatility of the past market occurrences and making the necessary helpful strategies and learning in your trading plan.

Holder: The specific owner of the contract is referred to as the holder in options trading.

Horizontal: This is a term describing the options of the same strike price experienced in different months.

Implied volatility: This is an estimation of the future likelihood market volatility by analyzing the market status through the current activities occurring at the options trading market. Some traders get to use this as one of their strategies the options trading market to acquire large chunks of profits.

Index option: This is an option contract where the index is the underlying stock and not shares of any specific stock.

In the money: All the strike prices possess some intrinsic value where for a call, all strike prices are below the equity price, whereas, for a put, all prices are the ones above the price of the equity.

Last sale: It is the latest price that a certain option trader has traded within options trading.

Long Option: This simply implies having purchased an option at online transactions and therefore own it.

Margin: This is a particular amount of loan offered by a particular broker of a specific trader during a particular trading period.

Mean: This is a mathematical operation where the total sum of observations in the market is divided by the particular number of observations in the market. The mean is used to provide data on various market values and the market standard deviation.

Open interest: This is the number of the option that has been sold and also the ones that have not been brought back or, in any case, exercise.

Option: It is a contract that allows an investor to purchase and sell a specific trading stock at a particular price within a particular period.

Option spread: It is established by buying and selling equal amounts of options of a similar class with the same underlying security. However, the strike prices and expiration dates of the options are different.

Premium: This is the amount of income received by an option trader as he or she writes a contract off to another party.

Put option: The kind of option where a buyer is given the privilege to sell 100 shares at a constant price before the expiration date. On another hand, the seller of a put option is required to purchase stock at a particular price if the trading option gets exercised at all.

Resistance: This is a particular level where the equity price cannot beyond any way higher, meaning that that particular price is the actual price limit.

Selling to open: This ideally describes the selling of a particular option to open a position.

Selling to close: Selling a close means selling a specific option with the desire to close a particular position during options trading.

Short Option: This means to have sold the option in an opening transaction.

Stock: It is described as a portion of a particular company belonging or ownership.

Spread: This is an option position established when a purchase of one option is established and a sale of an option too using the same underlying asset available in the trading market.

Strike price: This is the actual amount of price in which you choose to sell or buy options when you decide to exercise an option in the market.

Time decay: This is the erosion period when the value of time of a specific option diminishes as the expiration date reaches.

Time value: It describes the value to which time is attributable in options before particular expiration date is reached.

Trading platform: This is a general trading site that traders interact with while making trading moves, buying, selling, and any other trading activities. Trading platforms consist of various kinds according to different variety of interests, and a trader gets to pick on a site in which he or she is most comfortable with.

Underlying asset: This is the 100 shares of stock that are involved in a particular agreement during a specified time.

Vertical: It is a term describing the options of different strike prices experienced in a particular month.

Volatility: This is the actual fluctuation of prices of stocks in options trading where the stock prices keep rising and falling within time hence making it hard for traders to predict likely future activities.

CPSIA information can be obtained
at www.ICGtesting.com
Printed in the USA
BVHW090338220621
610126BV00013B/3093